A DORLING KINDERSLEY BOOK

Written and edited by Angela Royston
Art Editor Nigel Hazle
Production Marguerite Fenn
Illustrator Rowan Clifford

Jane Burton was assisted by Hazel Taylor

First published in Great Britain in 1991 by
Dorling Kindersley Limited, 9 Henrietta Street, London WC2E 8PS

A CIP catalogue record for this book is available
from the British Library

ISBN 0-86318-542-8

Typesetting by Goodfellow & Egan
Colour reproduction by Scantrans, Singapore
Printed in Italy by L.E.G.O.

SEE HOW THEY GROW
PUPPY

photographed by
JANE BURTON

DORLING KINDERSLEY
London • New York • Stuttgart

Just born

I am one day old.
I cannot see
or hear, but I
can smell.

I smell my mother
and crawl to her.
She feeds me
with milk.

This is me

Asleep in a heap

I am nine days old.
I sleep snuggled up warm
and close to my
brothers and
sisters.

I open my eyes
but everything is
a blur. I soon fall
asleep again.

Feeding time

I am two weeks old.
I am dreaming of milk
and I whimper and sniff.

I wake up. Where is everyone? Oh no! They are feeding already.

I climb over Mum and push in too.

Exploring

I am three weeks old
and I am growing fast.
I can see and hear and
walk very well.

Off I go to explore on my own.

Everything I find is new and interesting.

Playing with Dad

I am four weeks old and I have my own bowl of food. Dad is licking it clean.

Come on, Dad.
Play with me.

Oh good, now
he is ready
to play.

15

Play fights

I am six weeks old and much bigger now. I love to play with my toy rabbit.

My sister wants to play with me.

But she has sharp
teeth so I push
her away.

Now she is going off with my rabbit!

Ready to go

I am eight weeks old
and I am wearing
my new collar
and lead.

My sisters are playing tug-of-war with their leads.

My brother is trying to take me for a walk, but I don't want to go.

See how I grew

One day old

Nine days old

Two weeks old

Three weeks old

Four weeks old

Six weeks old

Eight weeks old

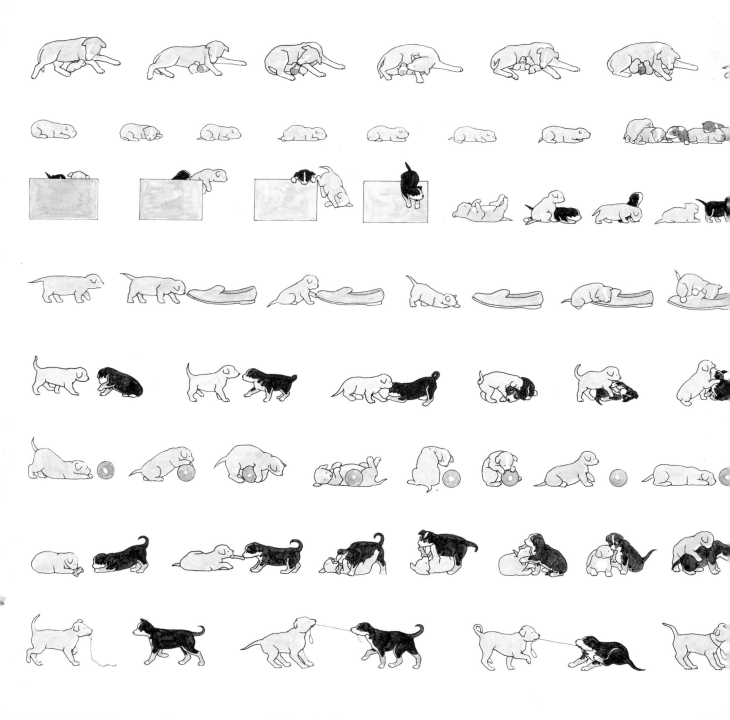